# *Inspirational Quotes for Life*

JEAN WATSON

authorHOUSE®

*AuthorHouse™*
*1663 Liberty Drive*
*Bloomington, IN 47403*
*www.authorhouse.com*
*Phone: 1 (800) 839-8640*

Published by AuthorHouse    03/12/2015

ISBN: 978-1-4969-7470-9 (sc)
ISBN: 978-1-4969-7469-3 (e)

Print information available on the last page.

Any people depicted in stock imagery provided by Thinkstock are models, and such images are being used for illustrative purposes only. Certain stock imagery © Thinkstock.

This book is printed on acid-free paper.

Because of the dynamic nature of the Internet, any web addresses or links contained in this book may have changed since publication and may no longer be valid. The views expressed in this work are solely those of the author and do not necessarily reflect the views of the publisher, and the publisher hereby disclaims any responsibility for them.

# About the Author

Jean Watson is a native of Raleigh, North Carolina, married with two children and one grandchild. Jean acquired her Bachelor of Science degree in business. She is a licensed insurance agent and currently employed in the insurance industry. Watson developed a passion for writing during her adolescent years. Her writings have flourished from simple love poems to words of inspiration. Jean views her writings as a gift and utilizes every opportunity to expose her talent. She is the author of *Poetry from the Heart, Poetic Expressions, Onyx the Butterfly,* and *A Thief in the Night.* Jean's desire is to share inspirational writings that will touch the hearts of her readers while also providing them joy and laughter. Jean believes her readers will find *Inspirational Quotes for Life* an inspirational tool to reach for in times of despair.

*My Family*

I wish to thank my husband, Winston O. Watson; son,
Brian Watson; daughter, Angela Watson; and grandson,
Aiden J. Watson. I dedicate this book to my brothers, sisters,
nieces, nephews, all relatives, in-laws, and friends.

# THE KEY TO GREAT FAITH

The key to acquiring great
faith is having the ability to
trust in things unseen.

## SOME THINGS ARE PRICELESS

Most things acquired in life have a price tag attached. The most important things in life that are free are common sense, knowledge, and opportunities. If you acquire one of the three, the others will fall within your grasp.

# THE SUN

The sun rises daily because God
promised the world light.

# TROUBLE

Since trouble exists everywhere,
your choice to avoid it also exists.

# REJECTION

Rejection can be beneficial, because it opens the doorway to determination, which leads to the roadway of success.

# NEGATIVITY

A person who displays a
negative character generates
a negative atmosphere.

# KNOWLEDGE

Knowledge opens the door to
opportunities and enables each of
us to create, inspire and lead.
Knowledge is free and
essential to survival.

# SEX

Engaging in sex because of
physical attraction is nothing more
than a moment of pleasure.

# JEALOUSY

Jealousy arises because of a
lack of confidence in oneself.
However, praise for your
fellowman emanates from a heart
that does not know envy.

# PEACE

Peace will not exist until it exists within the hearts of humanity. Only then will the world experience it.

# PLOTTING TO GENERATE FAILURE FOR OTHERS

You must practice extreme caution
if trying to set another person
up for failure, because eventually
you will become a victim of your
own destructive plotting.

# A FOOL

An intelligent individual would never leave his or her spouse for another person for moments of passion. Only a fool would do such a thing.

# ENGAGING IN SEXUAL ACTIVITIES

Love living enough to protect yourself. Love humankind enough not to jeopardize someone else's life.

# DEFINITION OF A REAL MAN

A real man lives according to God's commandments. He that does otherwise is just a boy.

# ADULTERY

Participating in adulterous activities hinders your ability to enter the kingdom of God.

# QUALITIES

Honesty, respect, and integrity
are qualities very few have.

# WISDOM

Wisdom is acquired strictly
through life experiences.

# LIFE

Life is the rustling of the leaves as
the wind blows. You will experience
the true meaning of life once you
show appreciation for the simple
things God provides daily.

# WAR

War will always exist as long as
people display a disrespect for
diversity and a difference of opinions.

## FAITH

True faith is gained through trust and not having to physically see proof that something exists before believing.

# A DIVINE POWER

If there isn't something, or someone, greater than each of us, who or what provides the breath of life and takes it away?

# LET GOD BE THE JUDGE

It is better to leave the judging of others to God, because people have no right to judge another if they have character flaws of their own.

# TO DRINK OR NOT TO DRINK

Occasionally it is fine to have a drink or two, but it is unwise to remain in a continuous state of drunkenness.

# A STORY VERSUS A LIE

There is a difference between a story and a lie. A story is written in a book, and a lie is nothing more than being untruthful and dishonest.

# GOOD OR EVIL

God gave each of us the knowledge
to distinguish between the two.
Your choice of action determines
what lies within your heart.

# COMMON SENSE

Plain common sense accompanied by drive, education, and determination are the key to success and financial stability.

# DIVERSITY

Diversity is change, differences,
and opportunities. It is a
wonderful gift from God.

# HELL OR HEAVEN

How you spend your earthly existence will determine which will be your final destination.

# CONFESSIONS

Confessions are great for the soul
and mind. Once they are out
in the open, peace settles in.

# JOY

Joy is a simple gift that is
generated through acts of
kindness, love, and laughter.

# HATRED

Hatred is an emotion that destroys
the good created by God.

## LOVE

Love is the greatest gift bestowed
upon the world. If it didn't
exist, we wouldn't be here.

# STRENGTH

Strength occurs when you recognize that you have the physical and mental ability to overcome your largest obstacle.

# HOW ARE YOU LIVING?

Your daily interactions with others and your actions toward humanity will determine the legacy you leave behind.

# DEATH

Living beings are destined to
succumb to death, but to live again
for eternity will be determined
solely by whom we serve.

# THE TONGUE

Sometimes a wicked tongue is
more devastating than a slap on the
face. Therefore, people should be
selective in their choice of words.

# NEGATIVE WORDS

Remember, whatever is in your heart will always find a way to rise to the surface. Whatever lies hidden in your heart will eventually show through your actions and verbal expressions.

# LIVING IN THE FAST LANE

It is not wise to speed down life's highways. Living life in the fast lane will eventually lead to disaster.

# EQUALITY

Equality is a word spoken
frequently by those who fail to
acknowledge its true meaning.

# ANGER

Anger is an emotion that spirals out of control and causes much devastation.

# LAZINESS

Being lazy and not utilizing the skills and gifts God gave you, because of a lack of motivation, often leads to unemployment.

# TAKING A CHANCE

Life is all about stepping outside
of your comfort zone to conquer
new challenges. You will never
know if you will excel above
any challenge until you take a
chance and follow through.

# SUPERIORITY

Superiority emanates from
negative hearts and minds because
of a feeling of worthlessness.
Inferiority exists because of a lack
of common sense to know better.

# BLINDNESS

Blindness is more than a physical handicap. Most people with physical sight are spiritually blind. Which is worse?

# THE EFFECTS OF BEING TOUCHED

Most people think of being touched
as a physical action such as the
touch of a hand placed on one's
shoulder or an embrace. Being
spiritually touched leaves an
everlasting effect in one's life.

# SKILLED VERSUS UNSKILLED

A skilled individual masters what he or she does. An unskilled individual lacks skills because of a lack of knowledge and training.

# A NEW BEGINNING

There is always an opportunity for people to change their actions, the way they think and live. Change brings about a new beginning, which enables people to view life from a different perspective and provides an opportunity to get it right the second time around.

# A WISE MAN

A wise man constantly seeks answers in different ways to satisfy his inquiries. The unwise man has a tendency to accept the first answer he receives.

# TREASURE VERSUS TRASH

The worth of a person's treasures
or trash is determined by the
imagination of the individual who
has either in his or her possession.

# BEAUTY

Internal beauty will always triumph over physical beauty. After all, an intelligent person knows that physical beauty is temporary, but internal beauty is everlasting.

# CURIOSITY

Curiosity is great for the mind.
It stimulates the brain because
it keeps you guessing.

# LONGEVITY

The key to longevity depends solely
on your faith, love, spirituality,
and the way you choose to live.

# RACISM

Those who sip from the cup
of hatred oppose and question
God's purpose for his creation.

# WHAT DEFINES A LADY

The true definition of a woman will not be determined by her physical appearance, what she wears, or her job title. Only her character will define who she is.

# LIFE AND EQUALITY

Life is a meaningless existence unless
equality exists for every living soul.

# VIOLENCE

Engaging in violence is nothing more
than an individual cry for help.

# THE FUTURE

Concerning yourself with what the future holds is a mental waste of time. If God wanted you to know, he would tell you. Trust that he knows what is best for your life.

# PEOPLE DON'T CONTROL YOU, GOD DOES

Do not hate those who stepped
over you to get to the top.
Remember, people have minimum
control over your life, but
God has complete control.

# YOUR SUCCESS DEPENDS ON WHAT GOD WANTS FOR YOU

Your success and future dreams may not be what God has planned; after all, he has the final say and determines what is the best for you.

# THE WORDS OF MAN

It is all right to listen to the words of men if they are positive, but be wise enough to know that you shouldn't live your life based on the words of men. Living your life according to God's words is more beneficial to you, because God will never fail you; man will.

# WORKING TO GET PAID

If you are working only to receive
a paycheck, you are selling yourself
short and missing opportunities
to pursue a promising career.

# WORK TO ACQUIRE THE DESIRES OF YOUR HEART

You must work diligently to acquire the desires of your heart and to fulfill your dreams. Depending on others to provide what you need is a total waste of time and puts your dreams further out of reach.

# A DECAYED CHARACTER

Although some individuals may be decayed to the core, that doesn't mean that all people are bad. We've observed the bad behaviors of others and see the destruction that derives from those actions. Using common sense and logic will enable humanity to seek a better resolution to benefit mankind.

# FEAR

Fear is a negative emotion.
Because of fear, many people
fail to achieve their goals, miss
opportunities, and lack the emotional
determination to rise above it.

# DREAMS

Don't wish, wonder, or focus
on "what if?" Blindly chasing
after dreams puts them
further out of reach.

# TEMPTATION

Temptation exists in every aspect of our lives. We must have the intelligence and determination not to succumb to it.

# CHILDREN

Although children are a
wonderful gift, they can
occasionally make parents endure
unnecessary heartaches.

# IDEAS

Ideas flourish through thoughts
and opinions. Once ideas converts
to action, the positive impact
on humanity is enormous.

# LOVE AND RESPECT

You must learn to love and respect yourself. Once you achieve that, you will display love and respect for humanity.

# A GREAT TEACHER

A great teacher displays a professional interest in ensuring that each student excels in the classroom, which prepares each student to excel in society.

# MIRACLES

Everyone searches for a miracle,
but no one wants to pay the cost
to obtain one. People constantly
call on God for help, but no efforts
are put forth to serve him.

# TEAMWORK

Teamwork is nothing less than a support system. Each individual within a team has his or her own unique qualities, work ethics, ideas, and solutions to offer.

# POETRY

Poetry is a verbal or written
expression that radiates from
thoughts and emotions that dwell
within the heart and mind of a poet.

# CHANGE STARTS WITH YOU IF YOU WANT TO MAKE A DIFFERENCE

If you want to make a difference in the world, you must engage in positive actions, assist others, and display love and compassion toward others. Only then will change take place within you. Once change takes place within you, humanity will benefit from it.

# DISAPPOINTMENTS AND LIMITATIONS

Life is filled with disappointments and limitations. The wise will acquire the knowledge to make each work to their advantage.

# SELFISHNESS

Everybody desires a wonderful life with financial stability, but often we are unwilling and too selfish to make the sacrifice needed to acquire that wonderful life.

# VALENTINE'S DAY

Valentine's Day is just another day. If one does what it takes year round to acquire love and genuine affection, there will be no need for all the commercializing and superficial drama.

# KNOW YOUR ANCESTRY

It is beneficial to know your ancestry, because it is wise to be knowledgeable about where you came from in order to transform into the person you desire to be.

# DESTROYING WHAT GOD CREATED

One must not destroy the life
of another. God never gave
anyone the authority to do so.

# DEATH DOESN'T DISCRIMINATE

No one knows when death may come knocking at the door. We do not have the option to refuse the knock, regardless of our race, riches, or mansions. Those materialistic factors have no relevance, because death does not discriminate.

# RICH MAN VERSUS POOR MAN

A man filled with the Holy Spirit is richer than one who is financially secure. Poorer is he who is financially secure, greedy, and craves only worldly possessions to obtain happiness. His knock on heaven's door may go unanswered.

# A TIME AND PLACE

Timing is very important when knowing when to act or speak. Sometimes we must let time enable us to let go of things that we cannot change through actions or verbal expressions. Knowing the right time and place often leads to positive resolutions.

# MOMENTARY FIXES

Momentary fixes are nothing more than temporary. Be wise enough to search the heart and soul for a long-term solution.

# BE YOURSELF

Pretending to be someone that you are not is fraudulent. Be content with yourself. Acting otherwise is an indication that you are not happy being you.

# HAPPINESS

Happiness comes from within,
never from material wealth.

# A PICTURE

A picture can be a beautiful image
but may also be deceptive.

# HUNGER

Hunger isn't just a physical
craving. People hunger mentally
for knowledge and wisdom.

# SURVIVOR

God provided his creation with the
knowledge and tools to survive by
supplying the essentials of life.

# EARTH'S LONGEVITY

Earth's longevity depends solely on
how creation uses or abuses it.

# PREFERENCES

The gift of making choices is
having individual preferences.

# DESIRE VERSUS NEED

Desire is an emotion to acquire
something for pleasure or
enjoyment. Need is acquiring those
things that are essential to life.

# ASSUMPTIONS

An intelligent individual never acts on assumptions. Only individuals failing to think through situations act on assumptions. An assumption normally increases the probability of an incorrect conclusion, which often generates an incorrect solution.

# BLACK-ON-BLACK CRIME

How can you destroy that which
is a part of you, your heritage,
strength, and support system?

# THE TRUE DEFINITION OF A "PLAYER"

A player has the characteristics of a child. He tries a variety of toys for momentary pleasure and enjoyment. Once boredom settles in, he becomes restless and bored with the old toys and frequently seeks out a different toy for enticement.

# COMPETITION

Competition is exhilarating when it works on the behalf of mankind. It becomes negative and evil when it generates harm to others. One must choose one's competitive battles wisely; not doing so will eventually result in destruction.

# WISDOM

The wise listen to and heed the words of the elderly, because they thirst for knowledge and wisdom. The unwise listen half-heartedly, with little interest.

# PHYSICAL LIMITATIONS

An individual who looks past his or her physical limitations will rise above them. Doing so will enable that person to reap the benefits of happiness and self-worth.

# DON'T BE CONCERNED ABOUT WHAT OTHERS THINK OF YOU

Concerning yourself with what others think about you inhibits your ability to unveil the true you. Use that time instead to please God.

# POWER

The power within you was handed to you as a gift. Use it wisely and keep in mind that the greatest power you can acquire is through spirituality and faith, never through money, fame, or physical strength.

# SAYING NO LEADS TO UNRESOLVED ISSUES

Do not be so hasty to say no, because saying no may lead to unresolved issues and unobtainable resolutions.

# GOD'S CREATION

We were created out of love and were given an individual uniqueness that can't be duplicated. Those differences are the individual identities that distinguish one person from the other. You should feel blessed that God created you the way you are.

# OPPORTUNITIES

Opportunities are similar to the rain: they come and go. It is very important to take advantage of every opportunity God sends your way.

# LIFE

Life is the color of a rainbow in
a butterfly's wings, the sound of
the rustling waves of the ocean,
and the beautiful glow of the
moon surrounded by a darkened
sky. You haven't experienced
life until you learn to appreciate
God's beautiful creations.

# DIFFERENCE BETWEEN A WOMAN AND A GIRL

A real woman displays honor and dignity in the presence of people she encounters, and puts a gleam of joy in God's eyes. Most men seek real women for marriage but use girls for momentary fixes.

# TO ELIMINATE STRESS

Drink a cup of love. Take a sip of
spirituality. Swallow a mouthful of
joy. Immerse yourself in a barrel of
Jesus. Engulf a box of blessings. Take
a glass of God's grace, and submerge
in a world of peace and tranquility.

# TAKE PRIDE IN WHO YOU ARE

Allow the world to appreciate the goodness that God has made.

# IGNORANCE

Ignorance is a trait man acquires and learns over many years, because it was not a part of God's creation.

# COMPASSION

Compassion flourishes
when the heart is pure.

# A POET'S PEN

A poet's power is in her pen, which reveals that which is in her heart.

# INDIVIDUAL DIFFERENCES

Being different is wonderful,
because God loves diversity.

# LIFE

Life is cruising on the ocean while watching a beautiful sunrise.

# CONFIDENCE

Confidence emanates internally from life experiences. You will not learn it from others or being in a classroom.

# THE EYES

The eyes reveal the true
desires of the heart.

# A GUITARIST

A guitarist's gift to his audience is the emotions he displays each time he strokes the strings.

# DISTANCE

Distance strengthens love between two hearts separated by land or sea.

# MARRIAGE

Marriage is successful for
those who take it seriously.

# HATRED

Hatred derives from hearts
never touched by love.

# TRANQUILITY

Tranquility is the sound of the rain tap dancing on a rooftop.

# ANGER

Anger can be a destructive emotion.

# TRUE LOVE

True love is not temporary;
it is everlasting.

# A VOCALIST

A great vocalist mesmerizes
the audience with angelic
vocals that generate chills up
and down one's spine.

# INSPIRATION

Inspiration is having the ability to touch the hearts and minds of others spiritually, mentally, and verbally.

# POETIC EXPRESSIONS

Poetic expressions are verbal or
physical displays of emotions
that emanates from the
mind, heart and soul.

# HAPPINESS

True happiness springs from
internal satisfaction with oneself,
never from external forces.

# SIMPLE THINGS

The simple things can bring internal
peace and joy. The touch of a hand,
a comforting voice or an embrace
can be a life altering experience.

# FASTING

Occasionally the body needs a boost of spiritual cleansing to enable the mind, body, and soul to open up and yield to spiritual healing and the voice of salvation.

# THE MOON

The moon is one of God's
wonderful gifts, providing light to
a world surrounded by darkness.

# LAUGHTER

Laughter generates joy and
increases longevity.

# WATER

When you drink the water of this world, you are drinking from heaven's fountains, provided to you to quench your thirst and cleanse you internally.

# BE COURTEOUS

How much energy does it really take to say good morning, hello or to speak to people you meet? It is more difficult to ignore someone than to acknowledge his or her presence.

# VERSATILITY

Having the capability to be versatile opens the door to the acceptance of change.

# IT ONLY TAKES A SECOND

In a second, unexpected
circumstances can occur
that can change life as you
may currently know it.

# A JOB

A job is similar to life; it is just what you make it. If you desire to have a job that is rewarding, you must put forth the effort to make your job more than just a paycheck.